Guinea Pigs Handbook for Beginners:

Detailed Guide on How to Effectively Raise Guinea Pigs as Pets & Other Purposes; Includes Its Care& Diseases; Feeding; Choosing a Breed; Its Home & So On

By

Markus J. Muench

Copyright@2020

TABLE OF CONTENTS

CHAPTER ONE 4

INTRODUCTION...4

CHAPTER TWO 10

    DEPICTION AS WELL AS PHYSICAL CHARACTERISTICS OF GUINEA PIGS PLUS SOME VITAL TO NOTE 10

CHAPTER THREE 15

    MORE ABOUT GUINEA PLUS THE DISEASES THAT AFFECT THEM 15

CHAPTER FOUR…………………………………………………17

ADVANTAGES AS WELL AS DISADVANTAGES OF HAVING A GUINEA PIG PET………………………..17

CHAPTER FIVE 25

   GUINEA REQUIREMENTS AND OTHER
   FEATURES YOU SHOULD KNOW ABOUT IT ..25

CHAPTER SIX 30

   PET AMAZING QUALITIES OF GUINEA PIGS
   YOU SHOULD KNOW 30

CHAPTER SEVEN………………………………………………36
REARING AS WELL AS REPRODUCTION OF
GUINEA PIGS 36

CHAPTER EIGHT……………………………………………..42

   DIET, HOUSING AS WELL AS MORE
   EXPLANATION ON THE DISEASES & REMEDIES
   OF GUINEA THAT YOU SHOULD KNOW 42

THE END……………………………………………………….54

CHAPTER ONE

INTRODUCTION

Guinea pigs are charming and cuddly, fuzzy and fun; however their proprietors will be the first to concede that thinking about them isn't as simple as it would appear. Like any living animal, guinea pigs require consideration and certain provisions to keep them solid and substance. While normal guinea pig life range is somewhere in the range of 5 and 8 years, an all around thought about guinea pig can live up to 12 years.

Fun and Lovable

Guinea pigs are charming pets who seldom chomp and who like to be held. Their interest and vitality make them engaging to watch. Give them a layer of sheet material on the base of their pen and they'll transform it into passages and homes, stowing away and springing up to the entertainment of everybody. Let them free in a room and they'll investigate each inch, making delightful photograph minutes as they totally dominate the corners, look out behind pads and snuggle with their people on the sofa.

Consideration and Exercise

Guinea pigs need practice day by day - in the case of going around the room or in a sheltered pen outside - and they should be firmly directed the whole time. Their interest and normal senses reach out to biting anything they can, including the family room sofa and force ropes. In spite of the fact that they can divert themselves in their enclosures whenever given enough toys, they likewise require day by day communication with their human pets, which can be tedious. Their little size methods little youngsters playing also generally can harm them; they're better pets for more seasoned children.

At first Inexpensive

Guinea pigs have generally modest in advance expenses: about $30 or somewhere in the vicinity and maybe less from a legitimate salvage association. At that value, it's sensible to purchase two, which is a smart thought. These social animals need organization. Two can play and stay with one another, a bit of leeway if their people are away a decent part of the day or don't have a lot of time to connect with them. Arrangement is moderately simple, as well - put 3 creeps of sheet material on the base of their new enclosure, include a food dish, a water container and some toys. They're all set.

Costs Add Up

Try not to try and consider setting aside cash by making an old aquarium their home. Guinea pigs need a pen for sufficient ventilation, with around 3 inches encased on the lower sides to keep the bedding inside. That enclosure ought to be at any rate 18 inches wide, 18 inches down and 3 feet in length for work out - 6 feet in length for two pigs. Bedding ought to be changed every day for a crisp smelling, clean home. Their adoration for biting methods they'll experience toys quickly.

Food costs include, as well - they need an exceptionally figured pellet blend, included products of the soil, grass roughage and a nutrient C supplement day by day in their water.

Guinea pigs, additionally called cavies, are individuals from the Caviide family, a gathering that incorporates a few types of rodents from South America. All cavies are social creatures that like to live in gatherings. The household guinea pig species, Cavia porcellus, doesn't exist in nature. Related species live in the wild on verdant fields and feed on vegetation including grass and leaves. Local guinea pigs are mainstream pets and significant examination creatures.

Cavies were trained in any event by 900 BCE and perhaps as right on time as 5000 BCE. All things considered, the trained cavies began in the good countries of Bolivia, Ecuador, and Peru. In these zones, Native Americans utilized them for food and strict purposes. Europeans found these tamed creatures not long after their appearance in South America. Cavies were first brought into Europe during the 1500s. Today, they are kept as pets the world over.

Guinea pigs are little, agreeable, 'loquacious' rodents. There are various varieties and assortments of guinea pigs, with a wide assortment of shading and coat lengths.

Ordinarily guinea pigs live for 5-6 years, yet some may live more.

Guinea pigs are generally thought of as great first pets for kids, yet it ought to consistently be a grown-up that assumes liability to guarantee they are appropriately taken care of and thought about.

Might you be able to give a saved Guinea pig a home? We salvage and rehome a wide range of creatures - including Guinea pigs. In case you're thinking about purchasing a Guinea pig for your family why not rehome one from us?

CHAPTER TWO

DEPICTION AS WELL AS PHYSICAL CHARACTERISTICS OF GUINEA PIGS PLUS SOME VITAL TO NOTE

Guinea pigs, as different cavies, are heavy and short-legged. Full-developed grown-ups run long from roughly 8 to 19 inches (20 to 50 cm). Grown-up guinea pigs are around 5 inches (13 cm) tall. The normal grown-up weight is 30 to 35 ounces (850 to 1000 g). Their ordinary internal heat level is 102°F to 104°F (39°C to 40°C). The guinea pig life range changes, however on normal they live 6 to 8 years (see Table: Guinea Pigs at a Glance).

There are right now at any rate 13 perceived types of guinea pigs. A portion of the more normal varieties incorporate the American, which has short, smooth hair; the Abyssinian, with short hair that develops in whorls; and the Peruvian, which has longer, plush hair. Bare varieties have likewise been created. Guinea pigs come in a few hues and shading blends, including dark, tan, cream, earthy colored, and white.

Guinea pigs' eyes are situated on the sides of the head, permitting them to see both forward and in reverse, in spite of the fact that they may experience difficulty seeing legitimately ahead. Their heads are dull and have little ears. Guinea pigs have 4 digits (toes) on each front foot and 3 on every rear foot. Each toe has a sharp paw. Their rear legs are longer than their front legs. They have no outer tail.

Guinea pigs have 20 teeth, including upper and lower incisors (for cutting and tearing), premolars, and molars. A guinea pig's teeth are "open established" and develop constantly for an incredible duration. Guinea pigs wear out their teeth by eating, biting, and pounding food. In this way, it is significant that your guinea pig's eating regimen contain an adequate measure of feed, grass, and grating nourishments to keep up solid teeth at the best possible length. Fat cushions in the cheeks, which are typical, can make assessment of guinea pig teeth troublesome

Uncommon Conditions for Guinea Pigs

Guinea pigs are agreeable just in the restricted temperature run from 65°F to 75°F (18°C to 23°C). They likewise incline toward a low relative stickiness (underneath half). At the point when presented to temperatures above 85°F (29°C), they may create heat stroke. Therefore, unique consideration should be practiced while shipping these creatures during freezing or exceptionally hot days. They don't flourish in drafty areas and ought not to be continually presented to coordinate daylight.

As a result of their little size, guinea pigs frequently endure wounds when outside their pens. They can be genuinely harmed in the event that they are stepped on or tumble off a table. In the same way as other different rodents, guinea pigs are pulled in to whatever looks intriguing to bite. Electrical lines are normal risks for these creatures. Different pets, for example, canines, felines, and ferrets, may effortlessly harm guinea pigs. What's more, numerous regular houseplants are poisonous for guinea pigs. At whatever point your guinea pig is outside its enclosure, it ought to be deliberately checked to protect it.

In contrast to hamsters and rodents, guinea pigs are for the most part diurnal—that is, they are typically wakeful during the day and rest around evening time. This settles on them a decent decision as pets since they will be dynamic during the day when you can watch them and handle them without upsetting their rest.

Keeping more than one guinea pig gives friendship to your pet. Keeping just guinea pigs of a similar sex keeps them from mating. On the off chance that you intend to keep male guinea pigs together, they ought to either be fixed or be acquainted with each other before they are done weaning from their moms. This will help forestall battling. Guinea pigs may freeze or become focused on the off chance that they come into contact with different pets, so keep them separate from canines, felines, or different creatures. This will likewise help forestall the spread of irresistible sicknesses.

Guinea pigs have irregular sensitivities to numerous regularly utilized anti-microbials when given orally, by infusion, or scoured on in creams. Huge numbers of the most generally utilized anti-microbials can be harmful for your guinea pig. Try not to utilize anti-infection agents or items containing anti-toxins on your guinea pig without the direction of a veterinarian

Understanding Guinea Pigs' Needs

There is nobody 'great' approach to think about all guinea pigs in light of the fact that each guinea pig and each circumstance is unique. It is up to you what you look like after your guinea pig, however you should find a way to guarantee that you address every one of their issues.

CHAPTER THREE

MORE ABOUT GUINEA PLUS THE DISEASES THAT AFFECT THEM

Guinea pigs are dynamic

Guinea pigs are dynamic as long as 20 hours out of every day and rest just for brief periods.

Guinea pigs are social creatures. In the wild they live in close family gatherings of 5 - 10 people, however a few gatherings may live in nearness to frame a settlement.

Guinea pigs' need a high fiber diet that is enhanced with nutrient C

Guinea pigs' eating regimen should be enhanced with a lot of nutrient C, as they do not have the protein expected to incorporate nutrient C and can just store nutrient C for brief periods.

Science and Diseases of Guinea Pigs

The guinea pig (Cavia porcellus), the main New World rat utilized regularly in research, has added to investigations of hypersensitivity, asthma, gnotobiotics, immunology, irresistible and wholesome illness, and otology, among others.

Maladies of worry that do happen in research provinces incorporate respiratory ailments (particularly those brought about by Bordetella, Streptococcus, and adenovirus), chlamydiosis, pediculosis, dermatophytosis, hypovitaminosis C, pregnancy blood poisoning, urolithiasis, horrible sores, dental malocclusion, ovarian blisters, and anti-infection actuated intestinal dysbiosis.

CHAPTER FOUR

ADVANTAGES AS WELL AS DISADVANTAGES OF HAVING A GUINEA PIG PET

Guinea pigs are among the less standard, however very mainstream pets that individuals like to save for different reasons. It isn't hard to make sense of the reason for their notoriety, yet a rundown of standard upsides and downsides can be recorded about them. Guinea pigs are mainstream rodents over the globe and are accessible in practically all pieces of the world. Here are a portion of the conspicuous favourable circumstances and inconveniences in the event that you are intending to get a pet guinea pig.

Aces for having a pet guinea pig

They are charming: This would presumably be the most discussed thing among pet proprietors who have a guinea pig at their home. They are charming and would really cause the proprietor to feel significantly better to have them close by.

They live more: A normal guinea pig has a future of around six to eight years which is an extraordinary thing. They can be incredible allies for little youngsters and can show them an awareness of other's expectations over some time. It is an extraordinary thing since they would remain around longer than a mouse or hamster.

Strong: It is a set up truth that guinea pigs are not exposed to any significant ailments and they have an incredible insusceptible framework to protect them. They infrequently fall wiped out, which additionally makes them safe around children and little children.

Friendly: They are charming and furthermore welcome the proprietor every now and again. Guinea pigs likewise will in general form a relationship with the family such that makes them a remarkable focal point of fascination in the house. Everybody would get glad by having it as their pet.

They are delicate: It is likewise one of their fundamental qualities that settle on them the most ideal decision to have as a pet. These creatures are amazingly delicate towards the family and don't cause ruin as a rule. They additionally will in general fall into schedules which would make them a perfect pet for most common labourers' individuals.

Taking them around is simple: Guinea pigs are little creatures and can move around effectively without assistance. They do require a greater space to run about for playing and getting exercise. In contrast to canines, they don't should be taken out each day. In any case, they can be hauled around effectively as a result of their size.

Veggie lover diet: Guinea pigs have a decent vegan diet and they can likewise follow a vegetarian diet effortlessly. This makes their waste canister much less rank than that of a feline or a canine. It additionally turns out to be a lot simpler to take care of them with a vegetarian diet that would be plausible and would cost less.

They are sensible: Guinea pigs happen to adjust quick and alter with their environmental factors making them a perfect pet for any home.

Consideration: Most of the pets require standard consideration or their conduct towards the family changes. Be that as it may, a guinea pig consistently stays in a similar state of mind and doesn't generally require a lot of consideration from their proprietor.

Discussing the positives, it truly gets the enthusiasm of an individual who needs to have a pet. Be that as it may, this likewise has its negative perspectives which are to be recorded also.

Cons of having a pet guinea pig

Space issues may come up: Guinea pigs will in general lean toward remaining inside the house instead of leaving it. This is the explanation that they need a bigger space that would keep them cheerful. They likewise go around which needs a greater space and with time they may get forceful because of absence of room.

Touchy animals: Guinea pigs of the considerable number of breeds are delicate towards vermin, worms and a couple different nuisances. They should be dealt with appropriately when any such circumstance comes up. In the event that they contract certain contaminations or get bug nibbles, it can make a portion of their hide drop out.

Homebound: As it was referenced previously, they remain at home for the most part and don't step out like canines or felines. This makes it convoluted for individuals who go out regularly to take it out with them. Circumstances in which the proprietor leaves the town would bring the need of portability for the pet.

They can smell awful: This is a typical grumbling among individuals who have been claiming guinea pigs or even bunnies. The confine when not tidied up every once in a while makes it stinky and unmanageable. It may likewise happen when a male guinea pig denotes his zone. This can settle on them an awful decision to keep as a pet on the off chance that you have an additional delicate nose.

Normally bashful: Guinea pigs will in general be timid and don't acknowledge their proprietor as effectively as felines or canines. This can be an issue for somebody who needs to have a pet for treatment purposes.

Loud now and again: They will in general make peeping commotions around evening time which may not permit the individual to rest. In the event that you are one of those individuals who love the possibility of a decent night's rest, embracing a pet guinea pig could make it harder.

They annihilate: These little animals can wreck a ton of things when they are separated from everyone else, and it would make a ton of difficulty for their proprietor to tidy up the jumble without fail. You have to ensure that they have appropriate things accessible for them to bite on and don't leave them unattended outside of their enclosure.

Costs: This is a certifiable worry for many individuals and guinea pigs go through it at first since their expenses are less. However, the vet charges, enclosure, veggies and feed would increment after some time.

Odd future: These animals become a necessary piece of the family rapidly and satisfy six to eight years which would wind up as a dismal connection story.

CHAPTER FIVE

GUINEA REQUIREMENTS AND OTHER FEATURES YOU SHOULD KNOW ABOUT IT

Guinea pigs can be exquisite pets, yet there are a couple of things you should know before making that enormous responsibility. From anticipated that life expectancy should the social idea of guinea pigs, here are a few interesting points before picking a guinea pig as a pet.

Pet guinea pig (Cavia porcellus)

While a guinea pig doesn't live close to up to a feline or canine, they're as yet a huge time responsibility. Guinea pigs live on normal around five to seven years, once in a while longer, so be set up to give care over the long haul.

Guinea Pigs Sitting Together

Guinea pigs once again are extremely social creatures and are at their most joyful living with other guinea pigs. Keep an equivalent sex pair to guarantee you don't have any undesirable litters. Females can be kept together, as can guys with no issues. Know that occasionally character contrasts in the creatures will mean certain guinea pigs won't get along. Presenting them as children is the most ideal approach to get a couple to bond, however even grown-ups can ordinarily be presented with care.

Guinea Pigs Need a Large Cage

Men Standing By Guinea Pigs In Cage

Guinea pigs need a great deal of floor space, and most enclosures showcased as test subject pens are excessively little, particularly for a couple. Making a custom made confine is extremely simple, however, and since guinea pigs are a decent size and not slick people, natively constructed confine is an extraordinary alternative.

Guinea pig looking out of his hovel

Guinea pigs make a particular wheeking or whistling type sound, regularly fully expecting getting a most loved treat or when needing some consideration. Despite the fact that for the most part not uproarious enough to pester the neighbors, a wheeking guinea pig can be shockingly boisterous. In case you're searching for a creature whose vocals will never intrude on an evening gathering or evening rest, a guinea pig probably won't be for you.

Guinea Pigs Are Generally Easy to Tame

While guinea pigs might be anxious or restless from the start, with reliable delicate dealing with, they generally become tame without any problem. Cautious taking care of is an unquestionable requirement, and youngsters ought to be directed with them, yet they are probably not going to chomp in any event, when pushed.

Guinea Pig Require Vitamin C

Guinea pigs are one of only a handful not many creatures (people are another) that can't fabricate their own vitamin C, so they have to get it from their eating routine. Picking a decent quality eating regimen and giving an assortment of new nourishments and roughage is significant, yet most proprietors decide to likewise give their creatures a nutrient C supplement. Vitamin C tablets are viewed as a superior method to enhance than adding nutrient C to your pet's water.

Close-Up of Guinea Pigs in Cage

Before taking off to purchase a guinea pig, check with your neighbourhood haven or salvages for guinea pigs needing another home. Numerous guinea pigs end up at covers and need another opportunity at an eternity home. Sanctuary guinea pigs are commonly social and agreeable. It ought to be anything but difficult to bond with a more seasoned guinea pig.

CHAPTER SIX

PET AMAZING QUALITIES OF GUINEA PIGS YOU SHOULD KNOW

Reasons Why Guinea Pigs Make Great Pets

Think stock

Considering getting a pet yet don't need the obligation of a feline or a canine? What about a guinea pig? Walk is Adopt a Rescued Guinea Pig month, so what better an ideal opportunity to get another pet and furthermore help spare a daily existence?

Guinea pigs, or "cavies," are short-followed, harsh haired South American rodents (family Caviidae). Guinea pigs have consistently been one of the fascinating pets I suggest most, particularly for families thinking about a pet just because. For what reason are guinea pigs one of my top choices? Here are 10 reasons guinea pigs make incredible pets:

1. Guinea pigs are tough. When thought about and took care of appropriately, guinea pigs are commonly extremely solid creatures. Like different pets, they can be inclined to specific

sicknesses — for instance, dental malady and bladder stones for their situation — however these conditions might be forestalled somewhat with legitimate nourishment and ordinary clinical tests. Additionally, since guinea pigs are from cool atmospheres, they don't do well in hot, moist conditions. Keeping them inside diminishes the probability that they'll overheat and additionally dry out.

2. Guinea pigs are anything but difficult to think about. They require roughage, new water, new vegetables and a modest quantity of pelleted food planned for guinea pigs, in addition to a nutrient C supplement every day. They likewise need a genuinely huge enclosure fixed with paper-based sheet material. The confine should be spot-cleaned day by day and totally cleaned week after week. Include some every day consideration and they are a great idea to go. Simply recollect, except if you need to wind up with a few minimal

extra guinea pigs, you'll have to isolate guys from females even before they are a month old!

3. Guinea pigs are incredible pets for youngsters. Not as delicate as hares and by and large less restless than littler rodents like hamsters and gerbils, guinea pigs are awesome pets for grade young children and more seasoned. However, recall, more youthful youngsters ought to consistently be directed around guinea pigs, similarly likewise with some other pet.

4. Guinea pigs carry on with long lives. By and large, most guinea pigs live five to seven years and some have even lived into their adolescents. This more drawn out life expectancy is significant for families to consider on the off chance that they are considering receiving a guinea pig, as you should be set up to think about your pig considerably after the children have grown up and moved out.

5. Guinea pigs are one of a kind. Numerous individuals don't understand this, yet guinea pigs

have a ton of character. Some guinea pigs are bashful; others are striking and prevailing. Because two guinea pigs look the equivalent doesn't mean they'll act the equivalent. Before choosing a guinea pig, make certain to cooperate with her to guarantee that her character lives up to your desires. For instance, in case you're searching for a cuddly pet, you'll need an active, agreeable little pig.

6. Guinea pigs murmur! Much the same as felines, guinea pigs make a calm yet discernible vibrating sound when they are cheerful, regularly when they are petted delicately. The vast majority who don't claim guinea pigs don't know about this lovable sound. Notwithstanding murmuring, guinea pigs make various different sounds including "wheeking" (screeching), "thundering" (a sound made by a male seeking a female), and teeth babbling (when they are irate or forceful).

7. Guinea pigs like to pop. "Popcorning" is a one of a kind conduct all the more normally found in youthful guinea pigs when they are glad or energized: They bounce up straight into the air again and again. Some guinea pigs run forward and in reverse rapidly, while others then again kick out their front and back legs. Numerous pigs likewise screech all the while. Popcorning is one of a kind to guinea pigs and is a great conduct to watch.

CHAPTER SEVEN

REARING AS WELL AS REPRODUCTION OF GUINEA PIGS

When all is said in done, veterinarians don't prescribe that individual pet proprietors endeavour to raise guinea pigs. It is frequently hard to track down homes with mindful and capable pet proprietors for youthful guinea pigs. Rearing regularly lessens the life expectancy of female guinea pigs. Reproducing a female guinea pig just because after she arrives at 8 months old enough can be extremely perilous in light of the ordinary solidifying of the pubic symphysis (a joint of intense sinewy ligament between the 2 pubic bones of the pelvis) that happens when the female arrives at adulthood. Sows that arrive at adulthood without an earlier pregnancy will most likely be unable to convey their young ordinarily. Caesarean segments are once in a while fruitful in guinea pigs in any event, when performed by a veterinarian who has involvement in guinea pigs.

Fixing or fixing of pet guinea pigs should be possible by a veterinarian experienced in managing little creatures, yet the medical procedure can be costly and conveys dangers. Fixing a male is commonly simpler than neutering a female. In any case, guinea pigs regularly don't respond well to medical procedure, sedation, or being kept in new environmental factors. The most secure, simplest, and most affordable approach to forestall reproducing is to house male and female guinea pigs independently.

In the event that you do choose to have your guinea pig fixed or fixed, search out a veterinarian who has effectively done countless these medical procedures. After the medical procedure, keep your pet peaceful and isolated from other guinea pigs while recuperating. A little, clean confine with towels for bedding functions admirably. The towels ought to be changed at any rate two times per day. Verify that the guinea pig is eating and drinking; additional nutrient C may likewise be useful.

Male guinea pigs (hogs) typically develop explicitly and can mate as youthful as 3 months old enough. Female guinea pigs (plants) regularly develop explicitly at 2 months old enough (55 to 70 days). In any case, the two guys and females can develop and be rich significantly prior. Females can have estrous or prolific periods whenever of the year, yet they are generally basic in the spring. The estrous cycle length is 16 days. A female is rich for around 6 to 11 hours, frequently during night hours. Female guinea pigs start another estrous cycle not long after conceiving an offspring.

The guinea pig incubation period is 59 to 72 days. The litter size reaches from 1 to 8 puppies, yet a litter of 2 to 4 is more normal. A female can bring forth up to 5 litters for each year. At the point when a guinea pig is going to conceive an offspring, any male guinea pigs close to her will accumulate around and attempt to turn into the predominant male so as to both secure the female and mate with her. The female has a short baby blues estrus that will keep going for just about a large portion of a day and, without a predominant male, the entirety of the guys will attempt to mate with the new mother.

Choosing a Guinea Pig

While picking a guinea pig for a pet, search for a creature that seems sound, stout, and caution.

The creature may at first be frightful or sketchy yet should, in a brief timeframe, react decidedly to delicate stroking. Check over the creature cautiously. The eyes ought to be splendid and clean, not hard or dull. The nose, eyes, ears, and rear-end ought to be clear and liberated from any release or staining. The teeth ought to be perfect and clean and the long incisors in the upper jaw should cover and simply contact the base incisors. Check the feet to be certain they are all around framed and move without any problem. The feet ought to be unharmed and without pieces, red spots, or scars.

Likewise, take a gander at the lodging for the guinea pigs you are thinking about. The confine or fenced in area ought to be perfect, with almost no scent. The creatures ought not be too packed on the grounds that this can prompt pressure and may reduce protection from ailment. Much of the time, guinea pigs will be kept in blended (male and female) gatherings. Since female guinea pigs can get pregnant as youthful as 2 months old enough, this frequently implies even a genuinely youthful female guinea pig can be pregnant at the hour of procurement.

Get some information about a prepurchase veterinary check. A capable seller will either permit a check by an outside veterinarian or will consent to acknowledge back an infected or pregnant creature that has been speedily inspected by a veterinarian. In the event that conceivable, have your new guinea pig inspected by a veterinarian before you take it home or as quickly as time permits from there on.

CHAPTER EIGHT

DIET, HOUSING AS WELL AS MORE EXPLANATION ON THE DISEASES & REMEDIES OF GUINEA THAT YOU SHOULD KNOW

Keeping more than one guinea pig gives friendship to your pet. Keeping just guinea pigs of a similar sex keeps them from mating. On the off chance that you intend to keep male guinea pigs together, they ought to either be fixed or be acquainted with each other before they are done weaning from their moms. This will help forestall battling. Guinea pigs may freeze or become pushed in the event that they come into contact with different pets, so keep them separate from canines, felines, or different creatures. This will likewise help forestall the spread of irresistible infections.

Guinea pigs have bizarre sensitivities to numerous usually utilized anti-toxins when given orally, by infusion, or scoured on in creams. A large number of the most generally utilized anti-infection agents can be poisonous for your guinea pig. Try not to utilize anti-infection agents or items containing anti-infection agents on your guinea pig without the direction of a veterinarian

Guinea Pig Cavia porcellus

Guinea pigs are social partner creatures that require day by day connection. They convey by making different sounds that have various implications and "popcorn," or hop noticeable all around, when upbeat. Incorporates smooth guinea pigs.

Guinea Pig Facts:

Diet

Herbivore

Diet

An even guinea pig diet comprises of:

Great guinea pig food, Timothy feed and constrained measures of vegetables and organic products.

Expect 30 to 50 mg of vitamin C day by day from great food, nutrient enhancements or leafy foods high in vitamin C.

Spotless, new, sifted, sans chlorine water, changed day by day.

Try not to take care of chocolate, caffeine or liquor as these can cause genuine ailments. Maintain a strategic distance from sugar and high-fat treats.

Taking care of

Things to recall when taking care of your guinea pig:

New food, Timothy roughage and water ought to consistently be accessible.

A constrained measure of vegetables and natural products can be given day by day, however ought not surpass 10% of their all out eating regimen.

Vegetables and organic products not eaten inside 24 hours ought to be disposed of.

Lodging

Guinea pigs adjust well to average family unit temperatures, not to surpass 80°F; be wary of outrageous temperature changes. The natural surroundings ought to never be in direct daylight or in a drafty territory.

A base 36"L x 30"W x 18"H break confirmation living space with a strong surface region and a lot of space for exercise and play makes a decent home for one guinea pig. It is ideal to give the biggest living space conceivable.

A naturally friendly environment is recommended and disintegrated paper bedding or hardwood shavings can be used as well. Cedar-based items are not suggested.

Guinea pigs might be kept in same-sex sets in the event that they are raised together; in any case, keep grown-up guinea pigs housed independently. Various kinds of little creatures ought not be housed together.

Ordinary Behaviour

Simple to deal with; inclines toward an everyday practice and comparative time for playing, taking care of and resting every day.

Stows away in objects, however will come out when individuals are close to the living space.

Bite on items to keep up the entirety of their teeth, which develop ceaselessly; guarantee they have a lot of bite sticks or mineral bites accessible.

Living space Maintenance

Clean and sterilize the environment and its substance in any event once every week with a 3% fades arrangement. Wash and permit to dry totally before setting the guinea pig once more into the natural surroundings.

Evacuate wet spots every day; change bedding in any event two times per week, or all the more frequently as vital.

Prepping and Hygiene

Guinea pigs remain clean and once in a while need showers, yet can be spot-cleaned with a sodden washcloth or unscented infant wipes if necessary.

Hide might be brushed with a delicate sponsored brush. Bare guinea pigs profit by a modest quantity of non-poisonous aloe-based cream scoured onto skin to keep it delicate.

Guinea pigs need their nails cut roughly once every month.

It is typical for a guinea pig's teeth to be yellow; cleaning isn't essential.

Talk with a veterinarian if a guinea pig's teeth or nails appear to be excessively long.

Wellbeing

Indications of a Healthy Animal:

-Dynamic, ready and amiable

-Eats and beverages consistently

-Sound hide and clear eyes

-Breathing is unlabored

-Strolls typically

-Conveys by squeaking

Warnings:

-Weight reduction

-Unusual going bald

-Loose bowels or messy base

-Upset relaxing

-Dormant

-Eye or nasal release

-Skin sores

-Congested teeth

-Normal Health Issues

-Medical problem

Loose bowels

Side effects or Causes

Free stool brought about by terrible eating routine, stress, inside parasites, messy lodging or different disease.

Proposed Action

Talk with a veterinarian to decide cause and treatment.

Medical problem:

Malocclusion

Side effects or Causes

-Congested teeth.

Recommended Action

Talk with a veterinarian to have teeth cut consistently.

Medical problem:

Parasites/lice

Side effects or Causes

Outside parasites that cause guinea pigs to lose patches of hair.

Proposed Action

Counsel a veterinarian for treatment.

Medical problem:

Ringworm

Manifestations or Causes

Skin disease brought about by parasite.

Recommended Action

Talk with a veterinarian.

Medical problem:

Scurvy

Side effects or Causes

A malady brought about by vitamin C lack bringing about helpless craving, sore joints and chest and seeping from the gums.

THE END

Printed in Great Britain
by Amazon